How I Got Off That
TREE LIMB

DR. GREGORY HARRIS

How I Got Off That
TREE LIMB

How I Got Off That
TREE LIMB

DR. GREGORY HARRIS

ARPress
ILLUMINATING IDEAS,
EMPOWERING VOICES

ARPress
45 Dan Road Suite 36
Canton MA 02021

Hotline: 1(800) 220-7660
Fax: 1(855) 752-6001

Ordering Information:
Quantity Sales. Special discounts are available on quantity purchases by corporations, associations, and others. For details, contact the publisher at the address above.

Printed in the United States of America.

ISBN-13   Paperback   979-8-89389-631-2
             eBook   979-8-89389-632-9

Library of Congress Control Number: 2024921474

INTRODUCTION

*Personal thoughtful recollection of things that
has helped me to get off the tree limb*

It was early one cold evening on January 6, 1960. This is the evening when I came into the world. I came early and before the time of my mother's 9-month delivery, but I got here before time but survived the early before time delivery. My mother told me that she was washing clothes, when suddenly, her labor pains began, and she had to rush to get to the hospital. Little did she know that her baby boy would have an early but on time delivery? At the time my mother was 22 years old and my father was 25 years old. My father had made a career in the military. My birth certificate reads, A1/c George Henry Harris 25 years Mississippi Armed Service Air Force and LaVenita Davis 22 Mississippi. How many other children are living 2, how many other children were born alive but are now dead? 0 How many fetal deaths? 0 Fetuses born dead at ANY time after conception 0, I came into this world at 4:58 p.m. My father often would tell me that I was not big as a tin can and I had to be carried on a pillow. At the time I was the 3rd child of three children born to George and LaVenita Harris. My older brother Tony and my older sister LaQuita, and there was me, Gregory Bernard Harris. I remember being at home with my mother. My family knows I have a memory like a computer. I always seem to remember things that everyone has forgotten. I am talking about numbers, names etc. I can remember one time when I had lost my delta sky miles card and suddenly, the numbers came back to me and I was able to get logged into my account on line and afterwards I found my lost card. I have always had to work hard and believe in myself. I am appreciative of the teachers that I had growing up at Harris Elementary in the McAlmont Community of North Little Rock, Arkansas. My first-grade teacher allowed me to use my God given talents to create bulletin boards for the classroom. One thing that I love about my first-grade teacher she taught us how to write our letters correctly. I can remember going into the bank and the teller saying to me, "I like your hand writing. My third-grade teacher had a funny thing to happen in the classroom. A mouse ran out of the closet, she jumped up in the chair and screamed. I guess that's why I was a little afraid of mice when I was younger but as I got older I grew out of that. The fourth-grade teacher made the students go to the board and work math problems but if the students missed the problem we would get a touch of that brown leather strap. This was the acceptable behavior in our schools in the 60's and 70's. Today they would call this class shaming. I guess that is one of the reasons I was afraid to tackle hard math problems. My fifth-grade teacher allowed me once again to use my creativity. I use that creativity to write plays and the students would act out my plays. One October I wrote a play about Halloween and the kids brought lots of candy as we went through the haunted house and from door to door trick or treating. It was fun to be able to use some of my God given gifts in elementary school. I believe that life is a journey filled with highs, lows, ups, downs, happiness and sadness. In the year of 1982 the Lord had instructed me to have a back to God revival meeting. At the time I was the president of our youth group at my church the First Pentecostal church under the leadership of Bishop Leotis Warren. I went to have a talk with my pastor to tell him that I wanted to have a revival meeting. The revival meeting was to only be for two weeks. I partnered with Johnny Hall our other churches young people president at Christ Temple Pentecostal church. The first week's revival was held at Christ Temple, a preacher from Baton Rudge Louisiana, Pastor Sanders was the guest preacher and the second week was held at First Pentecostal and a preacher from Montgomery Alabama, WW Tomblin was the guest speaker. I saw signs and wonders during this revival meeting and the preacher said to me, "Get off that limb." I was twenty-two at the time and did not really understand what the preacher was saying but he took the time to explain to me what he meant. He said look out that window at the tree. You see those apples on the tree. You cannot get apple pie until you get the apples off the tree, so he repeated, "Get off of that limb." This has stayed with me all my life since it was spoken to me and I have never forgotten it. I have other memories of school that I will share within this book, but I believe you can become anything that you want to become but you must be willing to work hard and commit to getting off the tree limb. Sometimes you must get a push from the winds of life to get you to get off the tree limb, but you get my point hopefully and you can begin to believe in yourself and know that all things are possible to them that believe. God has a plan for your life to give you an expected end and you can make it with his help. Remove yourself from negative people because this will only hold you back and keep you from obtaining all the things that God has already designed for your life. You are not a mistake and you are all that God created you to be. I have decided to hold my head up and push through adversity. I have decided that my life is a blessing. Even though I was born early and did not weigh much, God blessed me to survive and now I am 59 years old and I have never seen the righteous forsaken nor his seed begging for bread. I have been blessed by the almighty God and I believe in the super power of God and I believe that he can do anything but fail there is no failure in him. If there be any failure the failure is in me and in people of this world. I thank God for the personal relationship that I have with him and I have learned to stop and listen carefully to the voice of God; to hear him and take him at his word. He has never felled me. I am excited to write my story in this book. It's been a long time coming but I feel the time is now and I hope you will learn, grow and be uplifted as I tell my story of how I got off the tree limb? I have had my share of struggles and I have had my questions about tomorrow but through it all God has sustained, blessed and kept me with my mind sustained and connected to all the success and blessing God has for me. He knows the road that I take and after he has tried me I shall come forth as pure gold. You must have a little rain in your life so that you can appreciate the sun shine. The rain helps you to soak in all the things that you don't like about yourself and when the sun comes out it helps you to dry off the negativity and move into the positive. What you put into your mind will come out either in a positive or negative way. Therefore, you must be careful who you run with. If the people who are in your inner circle or not adding to your success you need to cut off the negative and move on to greater and more positive connections that can help you to get to the next level in your life. Jesus said, Take ye away the stone. Martha, the sister of him that was dead, saith unto him, Lord, by this time he stinketh: for he hath been dead four days. (St. John 11:39 King James Version). There are times when you and I must have someone to help us to take the stone away. Taking the stone away is just the same as getting off the tree limb. No matter if there is one other or a group of supporters to help you to navigate through the obstacles of life to help you to get through your challenges to go to your next chapter and your God given destiny. I am a true believer that God is in control of everything and if we put all of our trust in him and let him lead and guide us through the good and the bad we will somehow get off the tree limb and we will be able to help support someone else to get the needed courage to get off their tree limb. I hope that this book will inspire you to take a leap of faith into the unknown waters of life and allow yourself to take that needed plunge of faith, allowing God to lead, guide and direct you all the way to your next chapter of possibilities unknown in the unchartered waters called life. You can do more if you only get started. So many times, I thought that things that I was trying to accomplish were out of my reach. I learned how to trust God more than just trusting myself. I know to some people this may seem out of the norm but for me it is the way of life. I thank God for giving me strong faith and belief in him, and he has helped me to conquer many test and trials that I have faced in my life. Some of the test I passed the first time and some of the test I had to keep going through the obstacles until I learned that I could not do anything in and of my own strength and power. I had to acknowledge the creator of life. As I trusted him more he helped me to realize that he was with me all the time and that I needed to acknowledge him in all my ways so that he could direct the correct paths for my life. I continue to trust him day by day. I will not take anything for granted and I am appreciative for all the ups and downs that I have had. I try to learn from each mistake and pull myself up by my own boot straps and know that when a mistake is made, there is time for a lesson to be learned. This can only happen if we are willing to omit that we have errored and with the help of the Lord we can grow wiser and stronger as we take baby steps to make the needed changes in our life to help us to get off the tree limb. It is a simple statement that I take to heart and I can remember the preacher saying to me, "Greg get off of that limb." What are you going to do about it, are you going to stay on the tree limb of doing nothing are will you walk by faith knowing that you can and will make it with God's help. I don't care what you are going through as you read this introduction of the book, but I want you to know that you can make it because I did. I made it because there were others who helped me to realize that I could make it. Sometimes just one encouraging word from someone can go a long way with a person who is feeling like they cannot make it any further. My hope for you today is that your life prospers and that you find yourself doing what God created you to do in this world. One thing that has helped me the most is to tune out the nay Sayers and keep moving forward. You cannot get anywhere looking back at the negative things that have happened in your life. You cannot control every situation but one thing you can control, yourself. I remember one of my counselor friends made a statement to the students in my classroom. She walked over to the light switched and turned the lights off and then turned the lights back on. She asked the students who controlled the power switch. No one can turn off your power unless you allow them to turn your power off. Today as I write this introduction I reconfirm my own commitment to not settling for the status quo but challenging myself each day to be the very best that I can be and not allowing anyone to turn off my power. I know this sounds easy, but it can be accomplished if we take a small bite each day, we can eat the whole elephant. Getting off the limb requires thoughtful consideration of one's self and the ability to pray, study the word of God and ask him for guidance and strength each day. And don't be so hard on yourself, if you make a mistake get up and dust yourself off and try it again and again until you pass the test. I am glad that I serve a God of a second, third, fourth and on and on chances to make things right and to change the page to the next chapter of our life's journey. I have not always gotten everything right but for every trying moment I tried to learn from my mistakes and try with all my might not to beat myself up too bad but to take the mistakes as lessons learned so that the same mistake is not made over and over again. We are humans and we are tune to make mistakes so if we learn and grow from the mistakes we make, I would say that the mistakes were worth the lessons we learned from them. Don't let anyone take your power away just because of the mistakes you have made. In the world who can truly say they have never made a mistake?

CHAPTER ONE

How did I learn to get off the tree limb when I was faced with pressure from my peers in school and I discovered in sixth grade the love of the almighty God?

"For God so loved the world, that he gave his only begotten Son, that whosoever believeth in him should not perish but have everlasting life. (St. John 3:16).

It was in my sixth-grade classroom where another student and I had a disagreement. When my teacher left the classroom, the other students were saying things to get me to start a fight. I knew better, but the pressure was so great, so I gave in to the pressure. I don't know what the disagreement was, but it was not worth a fight. The ring leaders who were edging on a fight with me and the other student put an object on our shoulders and waited for the first person to knock the object off and then the fight broke out. I remember my teacher coming back into the room and the first thing I heard the teacher say, "Greg I am surprised at you". Then the teacher took me and the other student out into the hallway and we had to touch our toes and get a few licks from the wooden paddle that the teacher had. This was acceptable and used when I attended elementary school. This was my first and only fight that I had in school. I was a leader even back then. I was on the safety patrol and was the one that usually got to run errands for the teacher. So, this was a lesson learned to not be persuaded by my peers but allow myself to make the right decisions and not follow someone else opinions of what I should or should not do. I heard a preacher say, "Opinions are like noses everybody got one" I have learned to trust God to help me to get through the trials of life. In the fifth grade I wanted the kids to select me to run as King for our classroom. Each year in elementary school we would have what was called a Spring Tea. Everyone would dress up in there Sunday's best and the girl and boy from the different classrooms who raised the most funds for the school fundraiser were awarded the King and Queen of the school. There was another student in my room who was selected to be the King in our classroom, but he had not raised the most money. My mother is a true salesman and she sold the most ads for the Spring Tea Ad booklet. I did not know that I was going to be the winner until my name was called as the King of the school. A homemade king crown was place on my head and I won a watch. I was so surprised because I did not know that my name was going to be called. I have always had a competitive spirit and I love to win even until this day. I hate to lose but I am a team player but just hate to lose. I thank God for knowing that he loves me unconditionally and I have found peace in the mist of all the things in life that I have ever encountered. Allow God's love to change your heart from hate to love regardless of race, or ethnicity. Red Yellow Black and White are precious in the Lord's sight we are his dear children.

I am the image of my creator, and how can I say I love him if I don't display that same love for my fellow man. You should do the same and spread the love of Jesus Christ throughout the world. My fifth-grade teacher left the school early during my fifth-grade year, but, the other students and I were reassigned to another classroom teacher's class. I made it through the rest of the year. Growing up most of my elementary teachers was African American. I started school with a program called Head Start. I can remember going to the dentist and visiting the fire station. I started school around the year of 1965, I got the chance to go to school at the age of 5 because of my birthday and I would turn six before the school year had ended. Now I understand how some students who were not 5 by September the day after Labor Day and they would not be allowed to start school until they turned 5 years old. During my first-grade year of school my dad's mother passed away unexpectedly. I can remember my grandmother traveling to my home town of Little Rock, Arkansas. She loved to cook, and she could cook very well. One of the things my sisters and brothers loved for her to make is bread pudding. She would save the ends of white bread and place it in a container for a few days and when the bread was a little old or stale she would make this delicious bread pudding. My grandmother's bread pudding would fit in a square aluminum pan and we would eat and eat until it was all gone but she knew that we loved her bread pudding and she would make it often for my brothers, sisters and I. We got the news that our grandmother had a heart attack we were very sad, and heart broken. This was a tragic thing that happened when I was a very young child. The story that we heard is that our grandmother got up from her bed and she fell on the other side of the bed. We traveled to Louisiana to see some of our other relatives in route to my uncle's house in Utica Mississippi. My aunt could cook as well as her sister could. I remember eating some grits for the first time. These grits were yellow. Maybe some of you have eaten Grits and Shrimp in Georgia or California at one of your favorite restaurants. I know that I have had grits and shrimp in both states that I just mentioned. During the week before my grandmother's funeral there were lots of people who came by my uncle and aunts house to give their thoughts, prayers and condolences to the family of my grandmother; this is what usually happened in the black community. The body was brought to my uncle's house and the body spent the night in the front room by the fireplace. The children were in the backroom and all the adults were in the front room and spread throughout the house. I was taught to stay in my place as a child, so I knew not to be in the conversations of the adults. Today things are different you find the kids sitting in the rooms while the adults are talking and sometime the kids interrupt the conversations of adults. When I was growing up this was not allowed, and I think today some of the kids are getting away with what use to be adult conversations the kids stayed in a child's place. I am grateful for my upbringing and it has helped me to overcome and I believe that it also has helped me to get off the tree limb. To lose a love one is never easy but each day you learn to grow stronger and you cherish all the memories of your deceased love one. I heard a preacher say once after his wife had died after she had a long fight with cancer. It's not bad to die if you know where you are going. Jesus said, Take ye away the stone. Martha, the sister of him that was dead, saith unto him. Lord, by this time he stinketh: for he hath been dead for days. Jesus saith unto her, Said I not unto thee, that, if thou wouldest believe, thou shouldest see the glory of God? (St. John 11:39-40). Death is never easy when you lose the one that you love so dear. Losing my grandmother in the first grade was a very sad time for me. When I went back to school I was crying in my first-grade classroom and the students ask me what was wrong with me and I shared with them the news of my grandmother's untimely death. I believe from this experience helped to usher me into being a little afraid to go to funerals. I never would take on the task of being a pallbearer because I was afraid of dead bodies. My first funeral that I attended was with my uncle. He went to a funeral of a man who was killed by a train. My mother did not want me to go to the funeral, but I wanted to travel with my uncle, so I got permission to go by my mother reluctantly. When I came back to the house, they had to keep the lights on all night in my bedroom because I was scared to death. I kept visualizing the man in the coffin. The coffin was made from glass; it looked just like an Ice cream freezer. Not the upright kind you see in the stores today but this one was more like the size of today's caskets but made from glass.

When I was in the third grade my father and mother purchased a new home. My father was in the Air Force and after they purchased the new home my father got his orders to go to Okinawa, Japan. At one point my father thought about taking our family with him to Japan but my parents decided it was better for us to stay home. So, my father and mother asked my mother's mother Ruth Kendrick Davis to come from Jackson Mississippi to stay with us to help my mother while my dad was gone off to Japan to serve in The US Air Force. During the time that my grandmother came to live with us I have very fun memories of my mothers' mother. She was not tall in statue, but she was a powerful woman and didn't take any mess from anybody. You would not have to wonder where she was coming from because she always spoke just what was on her mind, especially if she felt she was being wronged or mistreated. I loved sitting down with my grandmother on my mother's side of the family because, she always had thoughtful things to say about her growing up and her family life and history. I am happy that I got the chance to meet my grandmothers on both side of my family from my dad and mother's side of the family. I treasure all the things that I learned as a child growing up each day, as I got a little older helped to shape, make and mold me into who I am today, and those experiences has helped me to get off the tree limb. We all can take those memories the good, bad and the ugly to help to sharpen and shape our life to help make us be productive citizen so that God may get all the glory out of our lives. Therefore, his sister sent unto him, saying Lord, behold, he whom thou lovest is sick. When Jesus heard that, he said, this sickness is not unto death, but for the glory of God, that the Son of God might be glorified thereby. (St. John 11:3-4). I had some amazing teachers from elementary, junior high and high school. These teachers helped to challenge me and to strengthen my skills so I could be a productive citizen in the twenty first century. I always wanted to become a school teacher. My father set the standard for our family to achieve our goals of being educated. My father retired from the US Air force and went back to school for his college degree. My father graduated in 1988 from Arkansas Baptist College in Little Rock, Arkansas. After my father graduated my mom and I got the needed courage to throw our hats into the ring to go back to school to receive our college degrees. I had been out of high school for ten years when I decided to go back to school to achieve my college degree. Before 1988 I had gone to some vocational schools but still was not totally happy in my present state so I made up my mind with help from my father to go back to school to be just like my father. I figured at his age if he could accomplish such a grand task, I could then follow within his footsteps. My mother and I graduated just like my father from Arkansas Baptist College in the year of 1992. I received my BS in Elementary Education and my mother received her BS degree in Business Administration. I started my career as a substitute teacher in the Little Rock, School District. I started subbing nearly every day of the week at different schools. I also got to go back to the school where I had done my student teaching to do a long term sub position. I subbed at Fair Park Elementary from January until March and then received another long term teaching assignment at Mitchell Incentive School that carried through until the end of the 1992 school year. I learned so much each day that prepared me to apply for my own classroom. I interviewed and was hired as a sixth grade teacher at Martin Luther King Magnet School in the Little Rock School District for the 1993-1994 academic school year. I had many opportunities to be a part of professional development, school leadership team, association rep, student council leader, association leader, write the school song, be involved on state committees and shape and sharpen the skills of my students. I also went back to school and received my Master's Degree in School Administration and recently received my Doctors Degree from Andersonville Seminary. From the time that my father graduated many from my family have gone on to get their college degrees. My father started it and we all continued in the footsteps of my father. My father passed away in 2016 after an illness from cancer. He is greatly missed but his legacy lives on in his children, grandchildren, and great grandchildren. Education has away to free you from clocking in and clocking out and you can have the opportunity to have a professional job. I can remember back when I was doing jobs that I did not like doing but they were the stepping stones to help me to realize that I could accomplish the things that I wanted to do in life. I really know and understand how important education is today. I wish that our elected leaders would give more attention to our public schools to make sure they have the funding that they need so the students can have smaller class sizes and have the best teachers and education support professionals no matter where the student lives. All students should receive a quality education regardless of their zip codes. It should not matter where a student lives. The teachers should be paid a salary so they are not working two or three jobs just to make ends meet. Teaching is a profession and teachers need to be paid just like we pay doctors and lawyers and other professional employees. I think that teachers are just as important and should be paid what they are worth so we can get the best and brightest to go into the teaching profession. I am glad that our elected leaders has made needed changes so schools are not just doing Standardized test with little or no growth for all students especially kids of color. I understand now more clearly what the No Child Left Behind was trying to do, it probably would have worked better if it did not penalize schools for kids who came to school already not on grade level. The teachers and education professionals were doing the best they could to help all the children achieve their best. One thing that I felt was wrong with the No Child Left Behind was trying to get all kids at the same level of achievement. If they did not come into the school on grade level and they had educational deficits it was no way possible that they would be on the same level with another student that was already on grade level or above grade level. The changes that have been made over the years have helped but we still have work to do. I believe that all children should receive a quality education. Schools from state to state have not received the needed funding from our elected leaders. Many school buildings need to be replace by new ones and some need to be completely redesigned and updated. It's easy to talk to talk but many who are making the rules need to go spend a whole day in a public school classroom. It takes special skills and a calling to be a classroom teacher. I am glad that I got the opportunity to live out my dream of becoming a teacher. I taught school for ten years and had my mind made up to become a principal. I went to school worked on my master's degree during the school year and over the summer months. I understand that life is a journey and you have many hills to climb to help shape you as you move forward with becoming who you were created by the almighty God to be. I have been blessed over the years to have many opportunities to reach for the stars. I keep pushing and pushing because if I was to get off of that tree limb I had to get enough courage to somehow push myself off of that tree limb. If I was able to push myself off you can do the same all it takes is your willingness to simply put forth the needed force and effort and push yourself right off that tree limb to success, happiness and blessings. You really are stronger than you think you are. All it takes is just a little push and I am giving you that push right now, can't you feel the wind pushing you to your next great chapter called destiny. If you have been sitting wondering what to do just make the effort to brainstorm what are your possibilities and start working on your goals one goal at a time. All things are possible to them that believe. So it really is helpful if you believe in yourself and start moving in the right direction to get off that tree limb. Many times we are faced with the difficulty of moving from a comfortable place to an unfamiliar place. It is in the unfamiliar place where you get pushed to the max to come out of your zone of comfort and move into those things that seem impossible. With man things can seem impossible but with God all things are made possible. If you can believe you can receive anything that you are willing to plan and pray so that God can continue to give you the energy and creativity needed to make things happen. It's time to get off of your tree limb and get to work. Do you have a plan and if you have a plan have you made any changes to it. How far alone are you in accomplishing your dreams? What are you waiting for? The clock continues to move forward it does not wait on anybody. It is time to make that needed change in your life and the first thing you need to do is to realize that you need to make the change so that you can realize what you were created to be and become. It is just that simple. A baker bakes, a singer sings, a creator invents, a doctor treats their patients and helps them to get better, and writers write the stories that become best sellers. What will you become five years from now? Have you done your work to make the needed changes? Do you know how to get started? These are questions that at some time or another people have had to address before they could get the needed courage to push themselves off of the tree limb. Will you be the next success story? We were all created with a purpose to live on this planet called earth. It is up to us to get off the tree limb don't wait any longer, get moving now! You are stronger than you think you are.

CHAPTER TWO

How did I get off the tree limb during the early years of my life that at times were filled with Joy, Peace, Happiness and Tragedy.

The early years of my life was filled with joy, peace, happiness and tragedy. I was the third child born to a family of seven boys and three girls. I knew what it was like to have brothers and sister around to laugh and to play with. We always found the time to play with each other and we had great love and respect for each other. In my early years before I was old enough to attend school I stayed at home with my mother. My older sister and brother went to school before I did. They were a couple years older than I. On one particular day when I was home with my mother, I was probably three or four years old at the time. We had a dog name Abigail and she decided that she would deliver her pups. As soon as she delivered her pups she would start eating them. They were small, cute, and black and white in color. She was even trying to put the puppies on the couch where I was sitting. I was very afraid because I never experienced anything like this before. It was a learning experience for me. I remember it as if it happened today. My first experience of school was when I attended Head Start at Harris Elementary School located in the McAlmont

Community of North Little Rock, Arkansas. I remember going to the dentist, fire station and getting an opportunity to explore many things. After Head Start I went to first grade. My first grade teacher was very caring and she allowed me to use my creativity within the classroom. Schools today have changed so far to the left that it is hard for educators to take the time that is needed to give some life lessons to their students. One thing that happened when I was in the first grade my grandmother passed away from a heart attack. This was an unexpected death. My grandmother would ride the train from New Orleans, Louisiana and come to Little Rock, Arkansas to visit her son, daughter in law and grandchildren from time to time. The last time she visited she applied for a job; while she went back to her home town to visit she had a heart attack and died. The job that she applied for called her after she had died to tell her she had been hired. I can remember going to my grandmother funeral There are more responsibilities being placed on educators and more and more evaluators are coming into classrooms to observe teachers and to give advice as to what, why and how things could change and be better for the students. I don't personally feel there is anything wrong with evaluators coming into classrooms to observe and offer supports for educators. I am simply saying that I feel it is just important to have heart to heart discussions with kids so that they can learn and grow concerning the things in life that are just as important as reading and math. I remember the No Child Left Behind that was introduced in 2001. And it started out punitive toward schools that were not making the marks that were needed to show growth. It was a hard task to accomplish to get everyone achieving at the same levels so there were so many changes that took place and today you do not hear anyone saying **"No Child Left Behind."** Since I was teaching at the early onset when the NO Child Left Behind legislation was enacted, I feel today that it would have been more effective to put things in place to support the special education students and those students who needed reinforcements in math and reading. All learners learn at different rates based somewhat on their past experiences and all students can learn and grow regardless of where they live or their zip code. All students must be given the same opportunities to learn. It is up our elected leaders on the local, state and national level to give educators the tools that are needed so that the teachers can be successful in meeting the needs of their students. It is sad that there is a shortage of teachers across the country and the colleges are not putting out the numbers of students who have majored in education like they did around 15 to 20 years ago. The teacher shortage will continue because the public stakeholders have downgraded the respect that educators so need and deserve. The pay is not what it should be and teachers give up a lot of their personal off the clock time to grade papers, prepare lessons and to research materials to support their curriculum. Educators have families as well and many times over the weekends they are missing out on quality family or me time to take care of things that are needed so that they will not be behind when the classes start up again after the weekend break. When will our elected officials pay teachers what they deserve? It is puzzling to me when I hear people say, "Anybody Can Teach" Teachers have a calling and everybody does not have the patients are the skills to teach. And those teachers who have put the time in to make a difference in students' lives should be respected by paying them what they are worth. Why do teachers have to work a second or third job just to make ends meet? Teaching is a profession just like doctors, lawyers, or nurses to name a few, The Teaching profession should be treated the same. I do not here of doctors or lawyers working a second or third job just to make an earnest living and to provide for themselves and their families. Hopefully one day we as a nation will wake up and put our money where our mouths are and give the needed support and resources to educators so they can be supported and not have to worry about their retirements, how to feed their families and other things that they should not even have to worry about. Teaching is one of the most important professions because they help to build our society with learners who help to shape our economy, health care, government, and social networks with the best and the brightest. Let's continue to advocate for laws to be past that will have a big impact on the teaching profession. And by so doing you will be supporting the future of America. Teaching is a hard profession and have changed over the years but I know a lot of teachers who are putting their heart and soul into the profession with little or no wage increases, little money going into their retirements and more and more changes coming from the government that says you can do this or do that, or you can't do this or that, Let the teachers get back to the basics of teaching the way that I was taught in the sixties and seventies. I learned a lot from the teachers who showed that they cared about me and my learning. I had teachers who pushed me to be the very best that I could be. This was important because those lessons that I learned from teachers helped to shape my understanding about life and the need to want to achieve at a higher level. I am grateful for teachers who cared about me and gave me life lessons so that I could grow and become a productive American citizen. There is nothing wrong with making sure that the students are receiving a quality education and that teachers are following through on diversifying the subject matter by differentiation of instruction and by adjusting the learning for those students who need extra supports. If our elected leaders, would carry the interest for education after being elected to office just like they talk about when they were running for office. Can't you hear the speeches concerning how important education is and what changes need to be made so that America's future generations can be successful in our nation's classrooms? It is going to take more than just words being stated in front of a group of supporters at a Campaign Rally to make the needed changes so that future generations of educators and students can benefit from our leaders paying teachers what they so deserve and providing the needed funding so that all students can get the resources that are needed so that they can grow and mature into productive citizens in our global economy. And yes, I believe that it takes a village to raise a child. What are you doing to make a difference in our schools today?

CHAPTER THREE

At the age of 15 I had issues with my vocal chords and went to the doctor week after week. It was scary to have to have surgery and be rolled into the operating room but it helped me to have unwavering faith in the face of unchartered waters of life. I believe and know that this experience helped me to get off of the tree limb.

I sung in the choir both in junior high, high school and church. I even remember when I was younger people tried to offer me money to sing. Some of the reasons I believe they would give me money is that I did have talent but I don't know if they realized how shy I was at a younger age. These experiences I believe helped me to grow and mature. I remember singing in church and would be very hoarse after I would finish singing. I was going to the doctor back and forth and many things were experienced before I had surgery to remove the nogoers on my vocal chords. One thing I remember the most is how some kids and school made fun of the way I talked. I always had a sort of raspy voice. Sometimes when I would go to a fast food restaurant to get fried chicken they would not get my order right because of my voice. When I would say, "I want two pieces or a leg or a thigh", for some reason the sound coming from my mouth was not clear to the listener. This experience was frustrating within it self because I was only fifteen years of old and it made me feel sad, and at times would make me feel a little unsure of myself.

I think it is important for adults to realize how to talk to kids. Sometimes what is meant well can beat a child down and cause them not be assertive and have the needed confidence within themselves to be the very best that they were created to be. I had my surgery and after I had my surgery I lost my voice completely. I had the faith that Job had after I had a loss of my voice God restored and healed my vocal chords. Today I sing professionally and God has been faithful. I have not had any more problems with my vocal chords and got a chance to travel around the county, appeared on Dr. Bobby Jones Gospel on the BET TV Network, sung for President Bill Clinton at a Democrat Rally in Little Rock, Arkansas during his second term running for president. All of these negative experiences I encountered with my vocalchord illness have helped me to push myself off of the tree limb. When I share my story of healing some people are a little surprise because they were not their when I was struggling just to believe in myself as a young teenager. If I had allowed what people said and did to influence my decision of being the best that I could be. I would not have had the experiences that I have had. It was no strength of my own accord. I know that God helped me to go through what I went through. It is what has helped me to believe I can do anything with God's help. I remember going to the hospital for my surgery. My parents bought me some new pajamas and they were there to support me through my surgery and my recovery. I remember getting hooked up to the IV, getting my blood drawn and going down for X-rays. They brought me a gown to put on with the back out and as a young 15 year old I was surprised. This was the first time I had been to the hospital since birth. I was born premature, and at 15 years of age had problems with my vocal chords and had to have surgery. Today I am grateful for those experiences because I really understand what the late great gospel singer Andrae Crouch was meaning when he wrote in the song entitled "Through It All." If I never had a problem, I wouldn't know that he could solve them and I never know what faith in God could do. Oh through it all... This is how I really feel that through all of the experiences that I have had in life helped to get me off of the tree limb. When I was rolled through those doors to the operating room and seeing those patients that were lined up on both sides of the room waiting for their turn to see the doctor they looked like they were dead lying in those beds. I did not know that they were under anesthesia; I just know that I was wide awake and it took a while for my anesthesia to put me to a deep sleep before my surgery. After my surgery I remember waking up fighting. It seemed as if I was in the boxing ring with Mahammad Ali and Joe Frazier. I was swinging but the nurse and my mother helped to calm me down in the recovery room. They were bringing me popsicles to eat but I was hungry and wanted food so the doctor allowed me to have some soft foods. My recovery had just begun. After my surgery I went home to continue my healing. It caused me to have a consistent prayer life. It also helped my spirituality. To see where I was and to see where I had become was the thing that made me feel good inside and to know that God could do anything. I am a believer of Jesus Christ the creator of all life from heaven he came down to earth and oh what joy that I have. It is so amazing just to praise my savior for all the things that he has done for me. If he did for me, I know he can do it for you. Believing is receiving all that God has for you to be made whole, healed set free and delivered. You don't know when and you don't know where what the Lord has done for me he gave me the victory and Yes, I am a believer.

CHAPTER FOUR

Falling in and out of love can have its disappointments, happiness and sadness but it's those moments that has helped me to realize what love is, what love does and how love with all its ups, downs, highs and lows has helped me to get off of the tree limb.

I have learned a lot over the years concerning love. I believe that every person wants to be loved and appreciated. I have had my share of falling in and out of love. Someone told me that I fall in love to quick. I fell in love with a girl in my high school; I truly loved and appreciated her. We went to junior high and high school together. We were both young and wanted what was best for each other. One thing that I loved about this person is the fact that they let me be myself. They told me that they would never get in my way and would allow me to use my creativity and continue being who I was created to be. I really feel that overtime we let the facts of life get to us. I at one point of time was the only one working and we started a family early. We were married in the year of 1978 and our first child was born in September of 1979. We were happy that we were blessed with a little girl. We both loved and nurtured our little girl and then without any plan my wife told me she was pregnant and we had a little boy in 1980. I was 19 years of age when my first child was born and then I turned 20 before the second child was born. I always believed in working and providing for my family because this is the way I grew up. My father always worked hard and provided for the family. I know during my early years I was just learning how to be a good husband and a great father to my children. I had lots of help from friends and family. I can remember crying when I did not have the money to purchase baby formula for my children. My family stepped up to the plate to help us provide the needed resources for our children. I believe this is the way that things use to be and people really stepped up to help young couples. I believe that my first wife and I out grew each other and we were moving in different directions. At one time I had gone to California and had a plan to stay there if I could work things out. I don't know what I was really thinking about other than wanting to be successful and provide for my family. I can remember staying with a friend and at that time I really did not know a lot of people that lived in California. I wanted to do better and have an opportunity to reach for the stars. I had ambitions even when I was 19 years old of being a singer. I can remember when my airplane ticket had a layover in Nashville, Tennessee. I started calling studios and a man from a studio named Alan Cash came to pick me up from the airport. He brought me to his studio. He had a white baby Grand Piano sitting in the studio. He listened to me as I played and sung. At this time a lot of people was saying to watch out for producers who were trying to take advantage of people. I believe this is one of those times when I missed the boat. When I arrived back home in Little Rock, the producer was calling me saying that he wanted to produce me. I had no manager and had very little knowledge of the music business. The producer was going to help me but wanted me to contribute to my own success. A friend had told me that if I was good enough the producer would pay for me to record. If I knew what I know now about any business not just the music business, I would have respectfully declined the advice given to me by a friend because if you are not willing to put anything into what you are believing that you can do what makes you think that a person will pay the entire bill to make things happen for you. When singers sign contracts they may receive upfront money but when the music is sold the upfront money is subtracted from the sales. I believe and know this was a lesson learned for me and I don't let people make decisions for me I make decisions for myself. Who knows today if I had taken an opportunity I may have been farther alone in my music career. Around 1990, I was divorced from my first wife. I found out after the divorce and just before paying child support that two babies were not my biological children. My grandmother use to say that one of the children that was born in 1986 did not look like me and the other child I was for sure was not mind because when the mother of the child became pregnant we were not on the best of terms and was no longer intimate as a couple so I was sure I was not the father. Later on in life the person I was married to asked me if I would forgive them. I decided to forgive and not hold any bitterness or resentment toward this person. Choosing to love and forgive has helped me to get off of the tree limb. I am not writing to say that I am a victim I am sharing my story in hopes of helping someone else that may have gone through the same situation or had similar issues in their marriage. I believe that marriage is a beautiful thing and I always wanted to be married and have a happy home. I find that marriage is a journey and it is something that you have to work at to accomplish success. I use to feel embarrassed because my first marriage did not work out as planned. I remember one day I came home from work and my wife and kids were gone. I saw signs of them leaving but ignored the new clothes that I saw in the closet. I was working and waiting for my wife to pick me up from work and she never showed up. After she did not show up to pick me up my thoughts of my wife leaving with our kids came true. I called my sister and a friend and they came to pick me up from work and to console me. I was not happy because the person whom I was married to decide to leave the state with our kids with me having no clear knowledge that she was planning her departure. I was very close to all of my kids and this caused me pain, sorrow and disappointment. You may say, wow how did you get through this trial? I only got through this trial with prayer, faith in God and belief in myself that I could move past this situation. It was around December just before Christmas when I found out where my kids were. I called my wife mother and she told me, "You have always supported our family and she gave me the phone number so that I could have contact with my children. When I called my children's mother she immediately hung the phone up. I called back and she said, "You now know where we are." I know that she was surprised to hear my voice. I could see if I was a wife beater, if I was not a good father, if I was the only reason we were not together then maybe she would have a right to leave without me knowing. I am glad that my children have embraced me and helped me to not feel that I was a dead beat dead. I know I paid my child support on time, I know that I sent gifts and there were times when I visited to be a part of graduations and other important events. I have had to put this behind me and move forward with my life. My kids are all a part of me and their mother and I am glad that they too have had to forgive, forget and move forward in their lives. One of my daughters when she was in high school told her mother that she had prayed and felt a leading from the Lord to come to live with me. This was a time for me to bond with my daughter. It was around 1990 when my daughter left alone with her brother and sisters to live in Tacoma Washington and she came to live with me in Little Rock, Arkansas 1999. That was about a nine year span. I have no bitterness and have moved on with my life. Recently my children had a 60th Birthday for their mother and they asked me if I would come. I came and was there to support my children. I have no ill feelings because their mother is the mother of my children and I am a part of their lives. If we constantly hold on to the bad things that happen to us we cannot move into the things that we were created and made by the creator to become and be whole, healthy and prosperous in our God given gifts and talents. Even though bad things happen to us I believe that overtime healing can take place even in the mist of situations that have caused us lots of pain, misery and sadness. Weeping may endure for the night but if you trust God and never doubt he will surely bring you out in the morning at the dawning your joy will come. After this situation I went about three years before I got married again. In this marriage I learned how to balance my checkbook and I learned some valuable lessons about money. The second marriage did not work because there was not true trust and commitment from both parties. If you are not totally committed in marriage it cannot work. No two people are just a like and it is a give and a take in marriage. Sometimes the other person just needs to be wrong for the sake of being wrong and you need to know when to say something and when to keep quiet when the time is right to present your issue or concern within the marriage. Sometimes when you get married and then you are divorced it can make you feel like, "What is wrong with me". It doesn't have to be that something is wrong with either party in marriage. It may be that the two parties never should have gotten married in the first place. After the marriage of my second wife ended I found that the phone had been bugged and there was clearly no trust why would the phone be bugged and I not know. I can also remember my wife telling me when I started working on my master's degree that she was not going to let me out do her and she then was inspired by me to get her master degree. I am not bitter but only sharing what helped me to push myself off of the tree limb. After my second marriage I felt that I would never be married again but a friend whom I knew some time ago we got reacquainted by going to a concert and I don't know why at the concert I was feeling butterflies in my stomach and the love triangle begin to turn on. I had just been divorced for the second time about three years and I ended up marrying again this time with a bride who had a grown son and two young daughters. This marriage started out ok but as soon as my children from my first marriage came into the picture there was trouble. I can tell you from experience that having a blended family can be hard. There are people today who have made a blended family work for them. If you are not willing to totally embarrass the children alone with your new spouse then don't get married because the marriage will end up most likely in divorce and you, your spouse and children can go through things that would have been avoided had you been honest with yourself. I know people have good intentions but really don't count the cost for their actions. When you count the cost for your actions you have to have a serious talk with yourself, and you have to be totally honest. Then you need to have a heart to heart conversation with your spouse to be; so that you can work out any issues within the blended family. If it is smaller kids you have to do your work prior to marriage and if you have adult kids you still need to have a conversation with them and workout common ground for dealing with your new spouse the love of your life. If these things are not properly handled at the beginning you will have problems that will help to end your honeymoon. I would suggest getting counseling from a professional that can help you to work through the difficulty and help you to create a plan of action for dealing with a blended family. This should be done before you say I do and after you say I do it should continue when needed. If you are not willing to put the time into having a successful marriage then I would tell you to wait until you are ready because once you say I do the clock starts to tick and you cannot backtrack on the things that you need to do to help and support you in your quest to have a successful marriage with or without a blended family. It is important to have marriage counseling before you get married and it is important when needed to have a professional counselor to help you to weather through some difficult times within your marriage. I can remember that my childhood pastor told me that he never called his wife a lie and they never slept in separate beds and they never went to bed upset with each other. They had a long loving and happy marriage. I know that I am not the only person to be married and divorce. Today more and more divorces are taken place. It never was my desire to be divorce. If I had the knowledge that I have today just maybe I would have made better choices in my decisions that I have to take total ownership of. Marriage can be beautiful. I was sitting on a cruise ship admiring a couple that had been married for 33 years. I observed the couple how the husband was taking good care of his wife such as helping her with her chair after dinner and walking close together as they shopped at the downtown outlet stores in the Cayman, Islands shopping area. It is good for the pastor that is going to do the marriage ceremony to take the bride and groom to be through marriage counseling. It is very important to count the cost and to do the work on the front end so that you can have a happy and vibrant marriage for a life time. I often think what could I have done different? What steps could I have taken to make the marriage work? I was working one Saturday, when I received a call from my daughter that my wife was moving all of the furniture out of the house. This all happened in 2002 I ended up going back to get my wife from Arkansas to reconcile in July of 2003. This only lasted for a few months and she had left again. We officially divorced in 2007 and had not lived together since 2003. I met another person in 2004 right at the time when I was ending the marriage with my third wife. The person was nice but all the drama I had gone through I know I was not ready to get back into a relationship and get married. I met the person through a friend we started by being friends. I had told the person that I would help them because they were working at night and did not have in family in Charlotte, North Carolina to help to pick their son up from school so I volunteered to help them by picking their son up from school after I got off work in the evenings. We were just friends from the time I met them in 2004 until I moved from Charlotte, North Carolina in 2007. I had made up my mind that I did not want to have a failed marriage again. I now see why people get a penult when they get married because if you have financial resources and you get marriage to a person and the marriage do not work you could be out of thousands of dollars that you will never get back. This happened to me twice when I had to divide my financial resources but the person I was married to did not have any funds to divide with me. One of my spouses received about 14,000 of my 401K and another about a year ago received over 100,000 of my retirement benefits. This person even knew that I was about to retire. I went to visit my mother and my wife of 8 and ½ years called to tell me that she was going to file for divorce. I thought she was kidding. When I came back home to Des Moines, Iowa she told me that I was going to receive a letter from an attorney. A few days had passed and she told me that I could go over to the attorney's office with her to sign the divorce papers. I really was surprised when I found out that my fourth wife had filed for a divorce. I prayed about it but felt that since she had filed for divorce, in my surprised I was going to allow her wishes to go through. I have moved on with my life. It was not easy and I had to stay strong in the mist of my storm and battle. My mom always tells me that, "A Heap See but A Few Know". I had to go through people talking, whispering about me when they did not have all of the truth but I learned that you have to remain positive even in difficult situations. When people feel that they know more about you, not because of what you have told them. It is only because they have one side of the story. A coin has two sides, heads or tails. Married people have to keep other people out of their business. It is not a good thing for married people to discuss their family situations with other people outside of the marriage. I am talking about in normal situations. A person that is being abused within a marriage needs to go through the necessary channels to protect themselves from harm's way. When you know that you have done the very best that you can you have to have the strength to move on and not beat yourself up and have self-deprecating thoughts about what you did or did not do right to save your marriage. I have learned to love myself and this has helped me to get off of my tree limb. I wish you the very best and wish you love and happiness in your pursuit of finding happiness and your soul mate. You have to become whole before you can help someone else. A lot of times we have been in bad relationships and moved from one bad relationship to another bad relationship. Don't look for another person to make you whole. The only person that can make you whole is the almighty God. He knows you from the inside out. Stop trying to find people to make you complete because you will be sorry in the end. God is the only one that can make your life full and complete. People will fail you every time but God will be there to pick you up and carry you when you feel your weakness and you can tell him all about your problems and he want tell nobody else. I'm working on myself and asking God to make me full and complete because I realize no person on earth can make another person full and complete only Jesus Christ has the power to do that. As you yield yourself totally to the master he will open up doors that you know not of. A woman does not have to go looking for a soul mate because the bible says a man that finds a wife finds a good thing. If you keep waiting your good thing is on the way. If you keep trusting God and know that he will make provisions for you. He will send your soul mate in a hurry and you and he will live a life of happiness ever after. This can happen if God is the one that makes the union. And to whom God has joined together let no man throw a sunder.

CHAPTER FIVE

Believing in myself and pushing when I felt I had no more strength to push forward has helped me to get off of my tree limb.

I started working when I was in the seventh grade. I helped a lady name Clara Shaw from my church to clean buildings and saved my money in a coffee can to purchase my first car. I had told myself that I no longer wanted to ride the school bus to school and when I moved to the tenth grade I would be driving myself to school. Just like I had said to myself and before I knew it, things happened the way I dreamed that they would happen. There is power in the words that we say the bible says that the power of life or death lies on your tongue. You can speak life or death into your own situation. One lesson I learned after I purchased my car and my car broke down and needed repairs. My father told me that the people that stick by you when your car breaks down are your real friends and the ones who leave you were only there for the ride. I was happy to pick up my friends and give them a ride to school. I was happy that I got the chance to drive myself to school. Its small beginnings that have helped to shape my thoughts in knowing that anything is possible to them that believes. I worked in a nursing home mopping floors and helping with the elderly patients in the ninth grade. I made a little more money and was able to contribute to our household expenses. Since my father was in the services I use to go to the Base Commissary with my mom and then my mom allowed me to go by myself to shop for our family groceries. I am glad that my mom gave me a chance to go by myself after learning how she did it. Today I have life skills that I learned as a child: how to cook, clean, iron my clothes, wash my clothes, wash my dishes clean, and many other life lessons that I learned when I was young. Being open to learn was another thing that has helped me to get off of the tree limb. I use those experiences to make me become a better person. The next job that I had was working in a grocery store called Piggly Wiggly in Jacksonville, Arkansas. I started out in the bottle room racking bottles and then I was moved to the task of making sure that the other young people who worked completed the task of cleaning the bathrooms, mopping the floors at the end of the shift and giving good customer service to the customers when we sacked their groceries and pushed the grocery cart out to their cars. I was chosen to be the store reporter and had the opportunity to write articles for the paper that went out to all of the stores from coast to coast. I am most grateful for the opportunities that God has allowed to come my way. Even though I have had some issues in my life the good has certainly outweighed the bad. I give God all of the glory for the things that he has done in my life. I never would have made it without him leading and guiding me all of the way through my ups, downs, highs and lows of life. Since I got married after graduating from high school I left Piggly Wiggly and applied for a job at Club Products International. This job afforded me health care benefits and I made a little more money. Since I had young kids I had to step up to the plate to provide for my family. I started out banding pallets during the day and cleaning the restrooms and the offices in the evening before ending my work day. I knew that I could do more and I wanted to do better. I felt embarrassed cleaning the restrooms especially when visitors would come to use the restrooms while I was cleaning. I felt this way because I was young and had just graduated from high school a few months ago and I knew that it was more in me. I am not putting down the job of cleaning buildings because it is where I first started working and was able to save enough money to purchase my first automobile. I am simply saying that I knew that my skills would take me further but I am grateful for my beginnings because small beginnings has helped me to realize that I was created to do more and it has been the thing that has kept me focus on doing more and more. One day I bided on a new job working in the warehouse shipping out cookware. The person that I started working with was a little older and she knew her job but was not at first welcoming to me when I started working with them to ship out the cookware by UPS, United States Postal and other shipping companies. It did not take me long to learn and the person was able to take days off and I filled the orders. I then got reassigned because the company was cutting one of the shipping positions. I was transferred onto the assembly line. I was at the very end of the assembly line. It was definitely not what I wanted to be doing for the rest of my life working on a job. The guy that I was working with at the start of the assembly line was very good at sanding the edges of the cookware as it traveled down the assembly line. Those pots would get hot and sometime would turn in my hand because I was not as strong as the other guy who had been doing the job for a while. I would be dirty when I got off of the job. I had a light blue Fairmont with White Bucket Seats. My seats would get dirty. I then moved to working at night in the Foundry. I did not like doing this job because it was working at night and many times on my way home I would be falling asleep trying to drive home. I walked off of this job and applied for another job working in shipping. After this job ended in 1985 I applied for unemployment. I received two unemployment checks and I have been working for thirty-four years. In 1985 I started working for Baker's Car Rental who had a corporate contract to do business also as Avis Rental Car in Little Rock, Arkansas. I started out washing cars and then I was promoted to an office job in Car Control. I had the opportunity to do the paper work for customers who purchased used cars for the Avis Car fleet, registered the new cars at the revenue office, put all the decals, license plates on the new fleet cars and other assigned duties. One thing I learned from my boss Tom Fazakerly is how to check my work over for accuracy. I worked at Avis Rent A Car for around 6 years in 1988 after my father graduated from Arkansas Baptist College my mom and I got the needed courage to pursue our career goals. It is never too late to start. As long as you have life in your body you can do anything that you put your mind to do. My mother and I started working on our college degrees in the year of 1988. We graduated together in May of 1992. I graduated with a BS in Elementary Education and my mother graduated with a BS in Business Administration. I had been out of high school for ten years but the courage that I received from my father is what I needed to help me to believe in myself and to believe that I could accomplish my goal of receiving my college degree. Just like I stated earlier I am a firm believer that you can do anything by working hard, keeping negative people at bay, praying and believing in yourself. The bible states that we can do all things through Christ that gives us the strength. I have strong faith in God and this has always been the force behind any new project that I have taken on or me going back to school to get my college degree. I can say happily today that I have Bachelors, Masters and a Doctors Degree. These degrees were not given to me I had to earn them with hard work and determinations. While working at Bakers Car Rental after I started working on my first college degree my boss told me that he was jealously of me. The negative comments that he made did not stop me from my pursuit of earning my BS degree in Elementary Education. I always wanted to be a classroom teacher. The teachers that I had in grade school allowed me to use my creativity to the fullness and I can always remember this was something I always desired to do. After teaching school for about ten years I had an opportunity to take training with the National Education

Association Intern program in 2000. I traveled to Washington D.C. for training and after my training I went to Binghamton, New York for a three month field experience in doing union advocacy work. After completing my field experience I went to Charlotte, North Carolina to work in a temporary six month assignment that turned into a fulltime position with the North Carolina Association of Educators. After working in Charlotte for eight years I applied and was hired as the Executive Director for the Des Moines Education Association. I recently retired after working in Des Moines, Iowa for twelve years. The Lord has been good to me down through the years. If it was not for the grace of God I would have never made it this far. I come this far by faith leaning on the everlasting loving arms of Jesus. When I felt as if I could not go any further he carried me until I was strong enough to stand on my own. I have had my share of life's ups and downs there have been times when I have been misunderstood. I thank God for all of the lessons that I have learned. I found out that knowledge is power and the bible declares that in all our getting get an understanding. We can sit and play all of the negative things that have happened to us over and over again but at the end where does it get us? I do not like to focus on the negative, I like focusing on things that are positive. If we spent more time focus on our dreams and ambitions we could move the needle forward. Some of us spend too much time talking about other people's business instead of minding our own business and moving ourselves toward our dreams and destiny. There is a saying that "A Empty Wagon Makes A Lot of Noise". I have learned to keep myself focus and center my positive energy on people who can help me not around people who are jealous and only looking for what's in it for me. I am still learning to trust God and not lean on my own understanding and in all my ways to acknowledge him so that he can direct my path. This is one main reason that I was able to get off of the tree limb. You have to trust God and let him lead, guide and direct your path forward.

CHAPTER SIX

When I had fallen how I got the strength to get up again. When I felt my weakest this is when the Lord made me strong and this helped me to get off the tree limb.

There have been times in my life when I felt like giving up. God has been my constant sustainer and inspiration. I have had a belief in God since I was at a very young age. My mother or no one force me to believe, I just know for myself that there is a God that rules and reigns. I grew up in church and always loved going to church. I took part in youth activities at my childhood church. My pastor always allowed me to use my gifts and if there were things that he would like for me to change he had a way of talking to you in a nurturing way so that you got the clear picture and you did not walk away upset but you walked away with a meaning of why something needed to be changed. My pastor Bishop Leotis Warren was a great example for our youth. He was an outstanding man within the community. He lived to be 99 years of age. I can remember the times when I would come to Little Rock, to visit him and always he remembered me even in his old age. The examples that was placed before me of hard working men and women and me taking the lead on the examples that came before me has help to shape my thinking and has helped me to get off of the tree limb. As long as I can remember I have had to fight within myself to be strong and courageous. I did not ask to be talented. I was created this way from my heavenly father. He endowed me with gifts. I make no apology for being able to do a lot of things well. I am a deep thinker and God has always given me big ideals too big for me to complete by myself. He has put people in my path to help make the out of the box dreams that I have had reality. I know what it feels like to have people trying their best to do you in so they can get ahead. They use their political correctness to step on you think that you are unaware of their selfishness. I know what it means to listen to the voice of God as he speaks to my spirit man and then follow through on what he tells you to do. There has been many times that God made a way for me to escape especially when my enemies thought I was casted down and could rise no more. God in his wisdom did me just like he did his servant David he moved me from the back fields to the forefront and for this I am grateful. I use to dream in high school that I would sing before thousands of people. God made my dream come true and today I am still perfecting the craft that God gave me to use. The voice that at one time was weak and feeble but God healed me and now I sing because I am happy. I sing because God has made me free. When I was young growing up I always listened to things that adults that were older than me said. I can remember a lady from my childhood church Missionary Powell, "I want to be hurt proof." This has stayed with me because there is always going to be somebody that will not agree with you, and there will be people who will be jealous of your gifts and will do all in their limited power to try to stop you. I found out that if you put your trust in Jesus he will make all of the naysayer's liars. Let everyman be a liar and let God's word be true. You don't have to worry about your enemies because in time God will take care of them. I am reminded of the story about the Hebrew boys, Sheddrack, Meshach and Abednego they were thrown into the fiery furnace but God delivered them out of the furnace with no injuries with a mighty out stretched hand. Many times we sit and wonder about things that we know we should be doing to make our lives better. We need to get up dust ourselves off and try it again. If you have failed the first, second, or third time it's never too late to begin again. The devil wants you stay down in a feeling for myself mode. If he can keep you down you will never get up to try it again. God is always standing by to help us with whatever we have to face. Remember the bible says that God will never put more on us than we are able to bear. I do not have all of the answers but I can tell you that some of the things that I have encountered have helped me to think outside of the box and to move myself every day to being more productive. Sometime the very thing that you go through is the thing that will help you to be stronger, and face adversities. We are really stronger than we acknowledge. If God brought us through before he will do the same thing again and again. Who told you that you couldn't make it? Who told you that trouble last forever? I have the answer for you the devil come to kill, steal and destroy. It's not the person it's the spirit of the devil that works within a person. So they are used to get you off of your game plan. To make you feel that you are not worthy to be blessed by the almighty. The devil will steal your joy and keep you with your head hung down. You are the one that has to deliver yourself from negative people. If the people you hang with cannot add to you then you need to dismiss yourself from them and handle them with a long handle spoon. Stop telling people that don't care about you all of your dreams and admirations. People that care about you will support you every step of the way on your journey to success and you don't have to be made to feel bad because of your God given gifts and talents. So as you get to the final words of this chapter. I hope that you will take a deep breath, get out a pad and pen and start writing a plan of action to get yourself off of that tree limb so that you are blessed, happy, fulfilled and successfully moving in the right direction to make a better you and become all that Christ created you to be. You just have to take one step at a time and finally you will be surprised at your happiness and success. To God be the glory for all the things he has done for me and for you!

Greg Harris is the author of two books, the first Jamie Noraa The Inspired Dreamer and the second book, How I Got Off The Tree Limb.Greg Harris is no stranger to the Gospel Music community. Blazing a trail from obscurity to prominence, Greg Harris has arrived with a brand new single "Ordinary People the Remix" Greg is a native from Little Rock, Arkansas. He grew up in the church and has always used his musical talents in playing the organ, singing and directing the church choir. In 1994, Greg formed The Little Rock Community Choir. Greg Harris and the Little Rock Community Choir traveled across the USA promoting their first project Songs from the Heart released in 1996 and Their Second Project Greg Harris Live in Little Rock released in 1998. Greg Harris and the Little Rock, Community Choir was featured on the Bobby Jones Gospel Show on the BET Network. The Choir had several hit songs from their first release that received heavy radio rotation and was listed on several radio stations' playlist. The songs lifted and inspired the people who heard the songs playing on the radio. In 1998 Greg was recruited to be on the program the city of Chicago presented to give a salute to the late Queen of Gospel Music, Albertina Walker. The choir shared the stage with some of the elite names in gospel such as the Chicago Mass Choir, The Barrett Sisters, and Rev. Clay Evans to name a few of the featured artist on this one in a lifetime celebration of a gospel legend. Greg Harris and the Little Rock Community Choir performed in Little Rock, Arkansas at a Democratic Rally for former president Bill Clinton and in New York City for the federal Government during the Fleet Week activities. Under Greg's leadership many inspiring musicians had opportunities to travel across the country and receive regional and national exposure. In 2000 Greg Harris took a break from gospel to continue his day time profession as an educator. Greg received Uni-Serv training from the National Education Association and was accepted as a 2000 NEA Intern. Greg did his field experience in Binghamton New York, while in New York; Greg continued using his musical talents by playing and singing at local churches. In 2001 Greg received a temporary assignment from the National Education Association to work in Charlotte, North Carolina. The assignment went full time and he stayed in Charlotte from January 2001-December 2007. While living in Charlotte, North Carolina Greg continued crafting his gift as he played in churches and sung with the Charlotte Chapter of the (GMWA) Gospel Music Workshop of America. The assignment went from 6 months to about 8 years.

In 2009 Greg was one of the featured artist at the Texas Announcers Guild Annual Conference in San Antonio, Texas. In 2010 Greg released the song Your Worst Is Over that received national airplay on various radio stations. In 2015 Greg was featured on Bobby Jones Presents on the Impact TV Network Greg is now ready in 2015 to take his music ministry to the next level He believes that the wait is over and it is his time and his moment to share the good news to everyone he can minister to, there is no stopping this Psalmist as he allows God to take him from small beginnings to the next level of his God given destiny. 2020 looks promising for the Sabbath Day Gospel Recording Artist. He will be celebrating his new CD release "That's The God I know" and his 60th Birthday. Also the release of his brand new Biography "How I Got Off The Tree Limb.

Gregharris365@gmail.com 501.343.8662
Facebook: https://www.facebook.com/gregory.harris.984
Twitter:@gregharris365
Instagram: dr.gregharris
Dr. Greg Harris
PO Box 1272
Rancho Cucamonga, CA 91729

www.ingramcontent.com/pod-product-compliance
Lightning Source LLC
Chambersburg PA
CBHW050908120626
46554CB00003B/1076